1 2 3

Carve a pumpkin with me

Elizabeth Gauthier

St. Clair Shores, Michigan

1st Edition

For information about permissions
please write Gauthier Publications at:

Gauthier Publications
P.O. Box 806241
Saint Clair Shores, MI 48080
Attention: Permissions Department

Frog Legs Ink is an imprint of Gauthier Publications
www.FrogLegsInk.com

Proudly printed and bound in the USA

ISBN: 978-1-942314-66-0

Library of Congress information on file

FROG LEGS INK

For Rigby

1 Pumpkin any size will do

Can't decide which, maybe get 2

Now is the fun part, you'll see thats it's true
let's think of all the things you can do!

3 Styles you could choose to paint

Zigzags to polka dots
they'd all look great

4 Hats and mustache combinations to try

With a beret, a top hat, or maybe a tie

5 Drawings of the face you should make before you begin

Some can be silly and some have a grin

Maybe your pumpkin's from
a sunny place

You pick 6 different sunglasses to try on its face

7 Different expressions
which one will do?

All of them are great
it's up to you

8 Different hats, which will you pick?

A king, a pirate, or
maybe St. Nick?

9 Nine different faces glow with candlelight

So you can see your creation on the darkest night

10 Friends come by to see.

Each one will ask
"Can you make one for me?"

How to draw a face on a pumpkin

Step 1: Sketch your idea on paper or you can trace a design that you find.

Step 2: Have an adult wash and dry off your pumpkin really well.

Step 3: Draw your design with a marker, have an adult help...pumpkins can be tricky.

Step 4: Color in your design with a marker or paint or let an adult carve out your design!

Step 5: Put out for everyone to see!

Choose a Pumpkin

Draw Design

This step is for an adult

Cut Out

This step is for an adult

Light with Candles

Draw your own Jack-o-lantern face!

(If this isn't your book ask for a paper to trace!)

Other books in the With Me series
by Elizabeth Gauthier

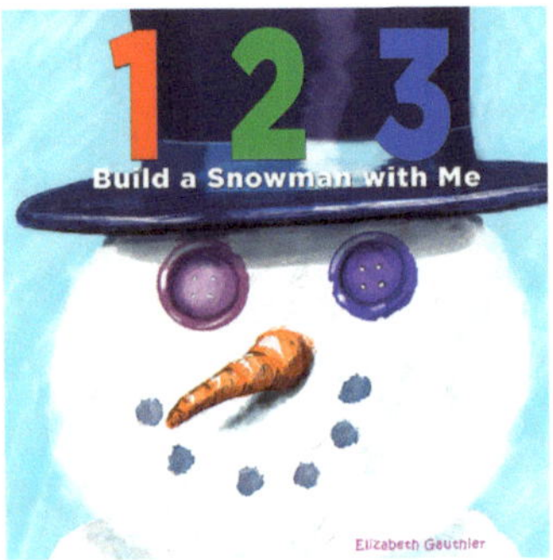

www.ingramcontent.com/pod-product-compliance
Lightning Source LLC
Chambersburg PA
CBHW040023050426
42452CB00002B/115
9781942314660